Misinformation, Disinformation, and Censorship

Heather C. Hudak

A Crabtree Forest Book

Crabtree Publishing
crabtreebooks.com

Crabtree Publishing

crabtreebooks.com 800-387-7650

 In Canada: We acknowledge the financial support of the Government of Canada through the Canada Book Fund for our publishing activities.

Author: Heather C. Hudak
Series research and development: Reagan Miller
Editor-in-chief: Kathy Middleton
Editor: Ellen Rodger
Proofreader: Wendy Scavuzzo
Project coordinator: Melissa Boyce
Graphic design: Katherine Berti
Photo research: Heather C. Hudak, Katherine Berti

Hardcover 978-1-0398-1518-6
Paperback 978-1-0398-1544-5
Ebook (pdf) 978-1-0398-1596-4
Epub 978-1-0398-1570-4

Printed in the U.S.A./072023/CG20230214

Library and Archives Canada Cataloguing in Publication

Available at Library and Archives Canada

Library of Congress Cataloging-in-Publication Data

Available at the Library of Congress

Published in Canada
Crabtree Publishing
616 Welland Avenue
St. Catharines, Ontario
L2M 5V6

Published in the United States
Crabtree Publishing
347 Fifth Avenue
Suite 1402-145
New York, NY 10016

Photographs and reproductions:
http://scholar.google.ca/intl/en/scholar/about.html—Screen Shot 2022-12-13 at 3.04.23 PM.png: p. 16 (bottom left)
Shutterstock
Amani A: p. 19 (bottom right)
arindambanerjee: p. 4
arogant: p. 16–17 (center)
Ascannio: p. 5 (top left)
Astrelok: p. 36 (top)
Bogdan Khmelnytskyi: p. 1
Everett Collection: p. 30
Evgenia Parajanian: p. 22 (center)
geogif: p. 19 (bottom left)
Karolis Kavolelis: p. 36 (bottom)
Katherine Welles: p. 22 (bottom)
Koshire K: p. 18 (top)
Nestor Noc: p. 35
Niloo: p. 16–17 (top)
photobyphotoboy: p. 34
PhotosWarren: p. 33
Rose Makin: p. 12
sdx15: p. 17 (bottom)
stockelements: p. 9
Sundry Photography: p. 19 (center right)
Tada Images: p. 16 (bottom right)
Thomas Dutour: p. 23 (bottom)
ValeStock: p. 20
Vladimir Tretyakov: p. 6
Wirestock Creators: p. 28
Zhenya Voevodina: p. 23 (top)
Wikimedia Commons
Alchetron: p. 37 (top)
Kaldari: http://allart.biz/photos/image/John_William_Waterhouse_14_Cleopatra.html: p. 14 (bottom left)
Charles Turzak: p. 10 (bottom)
Megalibrarygirl: p. 11 (top)
Soerfm: p. 14 (bottom right)
U.S. National Archives and Records Administration: p. 15
Virginia Association Opposed to Woman's Suffrage: p. 10 (top)
White House—Eisenhower Presidential Library: p. 24
www.archives.gov:research—Screen Shot 2022-12-14 at 11.55.05 AM: p. 21 (bottom right)
www.pewresearch.org:publications—Screen Shot 2022-12-15 at 2.25.51 PM: p. 38 (bottom left)
www.publicagenda.org—Screen Shot 2022-12-15 at 2.25.19 PM: p. 38 (bottom right)
Diagrams: Katherine Berti

CONTENTS

1 WELL INFORMED OR MISINFORMED?

In 2020, the entire world was faced with an **unprecedented** challenge. The COVID-19 virus quickly spread around the world, infecting millions and pushing health systems to the brink of collapse. In the midst of this, some people were looking at the advice of scientists with skepticism. How could they be trusted when their advice kept changing? Meanwhile, social media posts claimed the virus was a hoax. With so much information and misinformation, how was a person to know fact from fiction?

Information broadly deals with facts and how they are interpreted. Misinformation is inaccurate, misleading, or false information. People often spread misinformation without intending to. They believe it is factual and mean no harm by sharing it with others. However, misinformation can be damaging. One social media post on COVID-19 claimed gargling with salt water would kill the virus before it reached the lungs. It had no scientific proof to back it and could be harmful. People who thought the information was accurate might have stopped taking precautions that would actually help protect them from the virus, such as social distancing or wearing masks.

Disinformation is similar to misinformation, but there is one key difference. It is crafted in a way that is intended to mislead people. People who spread disinformation do so purposely. They want others to believe the story they give them so they can **persuade** them to think or feel a certain way.

▶ Misinformation and disinformation are differentiated by the intent of the person who creates or shares the information.

▲ Following the U.S. presidential election in 2020, then-president Donald Trump claimed the election results were rigged. He made false accusations of voting **fraud** in an attempt to overturn his defeat. There was no evidence to support his claims, but he continued to try to persuade people with disinformation.

> "*The unvaccinated are responsible for their own choices. But those choices have been fueled by dangerous misinformation on cable TV and social media. You know, these companies and personalities are making money by peddling lies and allowing misinformation that can kill their own customers and their own supporters. It's wrong. It's immoral. I call on the purveyors of these lies and misinformation to stop it. Stop it now.*"

U.S. President Joe Biden in a December 2021 statement about misinformation and disinformation spread on TV and through social media during the COVID-19 crisis

QUESTIONS TO ASK

Within this book are three types of boxes with questions to help your critical thinking about misinformation, disinformation, and censorship. The icons will help you identify them.

THE CENTRAL ISSUES

Learning about the main points of information.

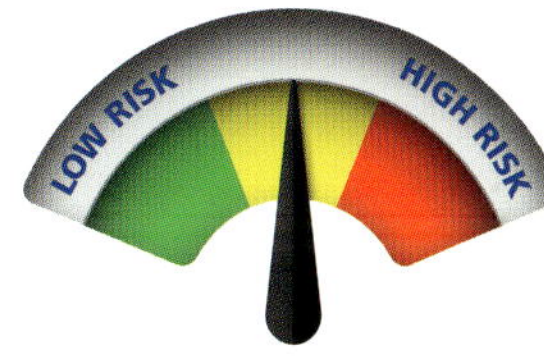

WHAT'S AT STAKE

Helping you determine how the issue will affect you.

ASK YOUR OWN QUESTIONS

Prompts to address gaps in your understanding.

▲ Censorship in the People's Republic of China (PRC) is required by the PRC's ruling party, the Chinese Communist Party (CCP). China has one of strictest censorship governments in the world.

Another way people control information is through censorship. It involves **suppressing** ideas, images, and words that certain people find offensive, dangerous, or **objectionable**. Anyone, including governments, churches, organizations, and artists, might censor information, such as TV shows, books, websites, movies, and radio programs.

For example, the Russian government is known to practice censorship to control how citizens think and feel about certain issues and events. In May 2022, Russia blocked access to Facebook and foreign media outlets. The government also passed a law that could put anyone in prison for up to 15 years for spreading false information about Russia's ongoing war with Ukraine. The goal was to make the government the sole source of information about the war and prevent any external or opposing points of view on the topic.

Misinformation, disinformation, and censorship can have a major effect on how people interpret issues and events. Sharing incorrect information or preventing information from being shared can cause harm by misleading people. Being informed helps us understand the world around us and how global events affect our own lives.

When getting informed about an issue, it's important to seek a variety of sources with different viewpoints so we can make well-balanced decisions. Once informed about issues, it's important to stay informed with the most current details. False information aimed at controlling the way people think and feel is difficult to counteract.

WHERE IS FREEDOM OF THE PRESS MOST RESTRICTED?

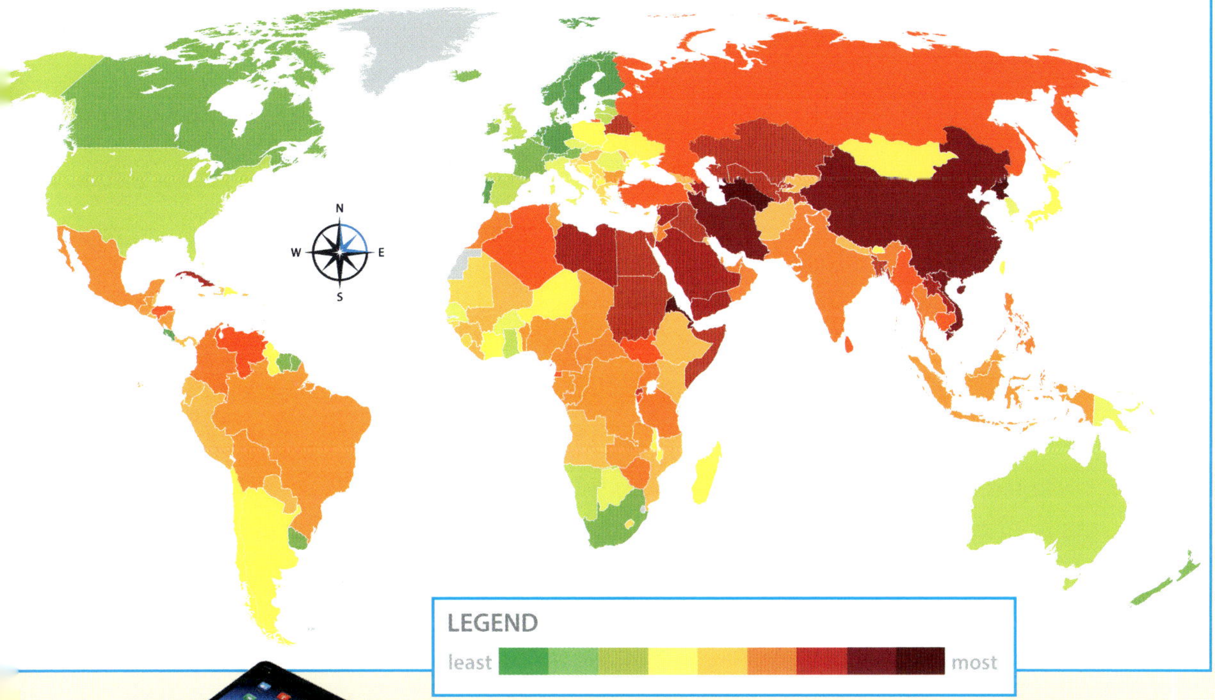

N
W
E
S

LEGEND

least — most

Source: rsf.org, May 3, 2022

THE CENTRAL ISSUES

Sometimes, people share false information. Have you ever encountered misinformation or disinformation? Where did it come from and what was its purpose? Did you share it with others?

> *We have to keep going—to document our country's war crimes for posterity, if for no other reason. Hopefully somewhere, sometime, someone will be held responsible for the terrible atrocities committed in Ukraine in our name. Hopefully, we'll still be around to provide the evidence.*
>
> Alexey Kovalev, investigative editor at Meduza, an independent Russian news site that was blocked by censorship practices

2 HOW TO GET INFORMED

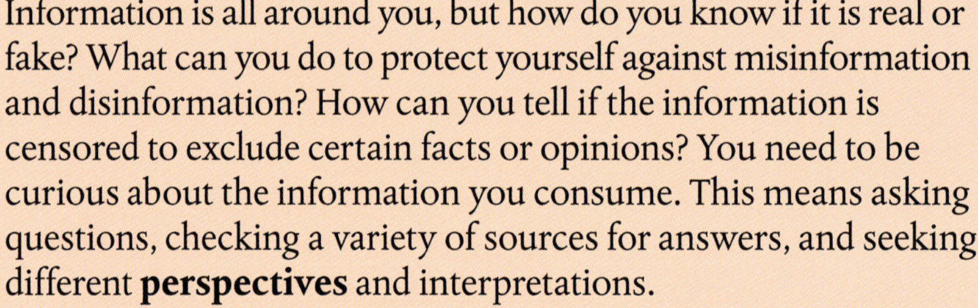

Information is all around you, but how do you know if it is real or fake? What can you do to protect yourself against misinformation and disinformation? How can you tell if the information is censored to exclude certain facts or opinions? You need to be curious about the information you consume. This means asking questions, checking a variety of sources for answers, and seeking different **perspectives** and interpretations.

BACKGROUND KNOWLEDGE

Having context can help you understand the circumstances surrounding an issue. It's important to find out when and how the situation came to be, any key players involved, and important events that have taken place. When you know the context, you have more clarity about the current state of affairs and can better interpret any information you consume.

Consider when the event happened and how that might affect any information from that time period. There might be historical elements that influenced people's thoughts and behaviors, such as **abolition**, women's **suffrage**, world wars, and **prohibition**. If the situation is ongoing, what is happening in the world right now? Cuban **civil liberties**, women's rights in Iran, and the Black Lives Matter movement are examples of recent events that might affect how people think, feel, and behave, and influence any information sources they produce.

Think about whether there are cultural, religious, or political factors that might have influenced content creators. Did the words they use have the same meanings as they do today? Were there different expectations for gender roles? How did people dress? All these factors can affect how we view information sources in context.

▲ Investigating the credibility of information often requires cross-referencing many sources.

▲ A television news reporter interviews activists at a Black Lives Matter rally. First-person interviews are one source of information. Like all information sources, news can reflect the slant, or bias, of reporters or of the news source.

LOOKING FOR INFORMATION

To build background knowledge, you need to look for relevant, **credible** information sources. But where do you begin when there is so much information available today?

The Internet is a good place to start. A targeted Internet search for your topic will provide links to organizations, experts, blogs, podcasts, newspapers, social media, and other information that can help answer your questions. But be mindful of the fact that anyone can post on the Internet, so the information is unfiltered. You do not need to be an expert or have any qualifications to share information about a topic. The content on personal websites, blog posts, and **open-source** encyclopedias might not be **vetted** for accuracy, edited, or fact checked. Much of what you find will contain misinformation and disinformation or omit certain facts or details. For the most credible information, visit websites published by university and research centers, governments, nongovernmental organizations, and subject matter experts.

You might also need to find other sources of information to round out your research and provide verifiable facts on the topic. The library contains all kinds of information, including international magazines, educational books, CDs, historical archives, and photographs. Librarians can help you discover appropriate information sources to help research your topic.

SOURCES OF INFORMATION

There are three main types of information:

Primary sources

These are first-hand accounts, original works, or direct evidence that are created by people who have personal experience with the subject. Speeches, photographs, e-mails, artwork, autobiographies, and survey results are examples of primary sources. They are created during or around the time of the event. The Time and Place Rule states that the closer in time and place the creator and source were to an event, the more reliable the information.

Secondary sources

These are based on primary sources and are created after the event takes place—sometimes many years later. The creator analyzes and interprets other sources of information to describe, review, or critique the event. Examples of secondary sources include textbooks, editorial articles, biographies, and journals.

Tertiary sources

These are compilations of other information sources. They often provide lists, indexes, and summaries of where to look for more detailed information. Dictionaries, databases, bibliographies, and encyclopedias are tertiary sources.

Sometimes, information is presented visually in the form of graphs and charts. Visual information is easier to interpret and understand. It can help make sense of complex information.

Anti-Suffrage Arguments
DANGER!

WOMAN'S SUFFRAGE THE VANGUARD OF SOCIALISM

Proof.—See here—

1. What is Socialism?
Socialism is against Christian marriage.
Socialism is against the Christian family.
Socialism is against the holding of private property.
Socialism is against Christianity.
Socialism is against the Bible.

2. If you hold your marriage, your family life, your home, your religion, as sacred, dear and inviolate, to be preserved for yourself, and for your children, for all time, then work with all your might against Socialism's vanguard—Woman's Suffrage.

3. In a parade in New York City last November they openly marched together. The Woman Suffragists as the vanguard, with their yellow flags. The Socialists behind with their red flags.

4. The Socialist red flag had this inscription: "Every Socialist is a Woman Suffragist."
Does every Virginia Woman Suffragist intend to be a Socialist?

5. We hope not. But "There is a way which seemeth right unto a man, but the end thereof is death."
Danger lies ahead of you.

Do you not recognize the kinship?
Is not this Plain enough for you?

Literature can be obtained free of cost at
Meyers Book Store, First and Broad Streets
Bell Book and Stationery Co., 914 E. Main Street

Virginia Association Opposed to Woman's Suffrage

PRIMARY SOURCE

SECONDARY SOURCE

PRIMARY SOURCE

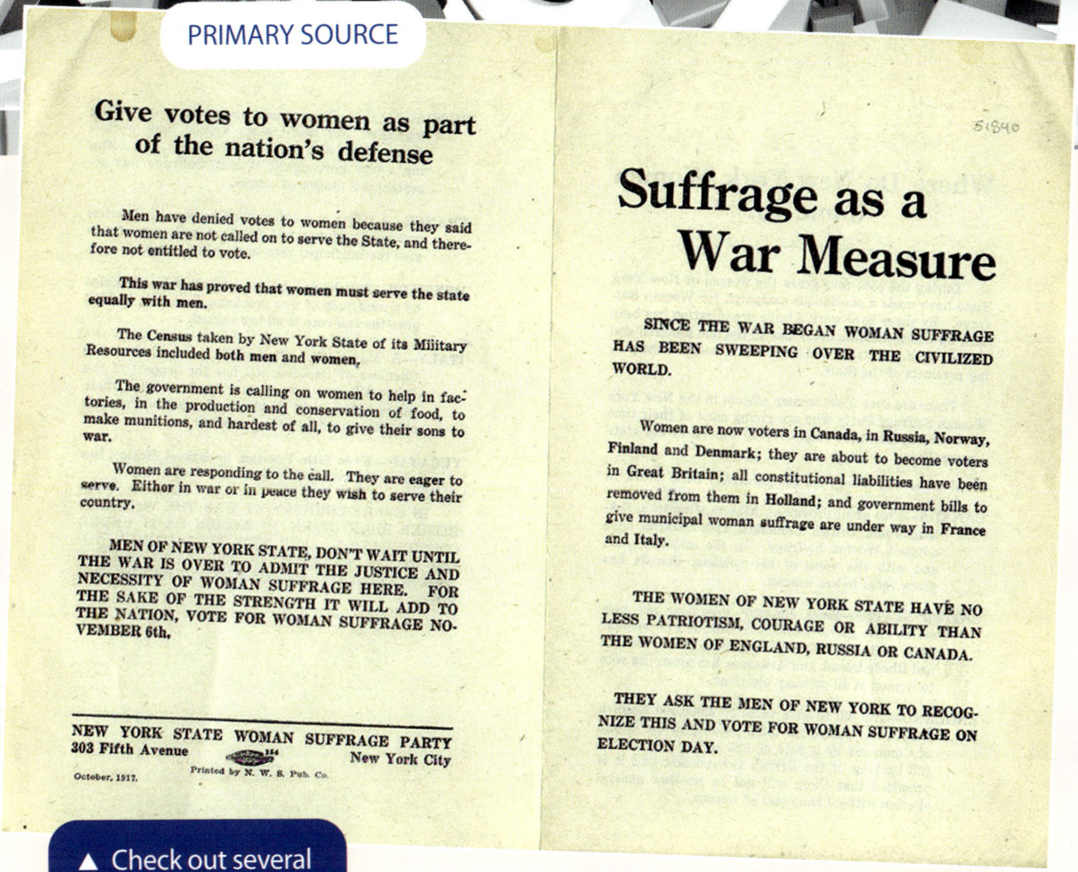

Give votes to women as part of the nation's defense

Men have denied votes to women because they said that women are not called on to serve the State, and therefore not entitled to vote.

This war has proved that women must serve the state equally with men.

The Census taken by New York State of its Military Resources included both men and women.

The government is calling on women to help in factories, in the production and conservation of food, to make munitions, and hardest of all, to give their sons to war.

Women are responding to the call. They are eager to serve. Either in war or in peace they wish to serve their country.

MEN OF NEW YORK STATE, DON'T WAIT UNTIL THE WAR IS OVER TO ADMIT THE JUSTICE AND NECESSITY OF WOMAN SUFFRAGE HERE. FOR THE SAKE OF THE STRENGTH IT WILL ADD TO THE NATION, VOTE FOR WOMAN SUFFRAGE NOVEMBER 6th.

NEW YORK STATE WOMAN SUFFRAGE PARTY
303 Fifth Avenue New York City

October, 1917. Printed by N. W. S. Pub. Co.

51840

Suffrage as a War Measure

SINCE THE WAR BEGAN WOMAN SUFFRAGE HAS BEEN SWEEPING OVER THE CIVILIZED WORLD.

Women are now voters in Canada, in Russia, Norway, Finland and Denmark; they are about to become voters in Great Britain; all constitutional liabilities have been removed from them in Holland; and government bills to give municipal woman suffrage are under way in France and Italy.

THE WOMEN OF NEW YORK STATE HAVE NO LESS PATRIOTISM, COURAGE OR ABILITY THAN THE WOMEN OF ENGLAND, RUSSIA OR CANADA.

THEY ASK THE MEN OF NEW YORK TO RECOGNIZE THIS AND VOTE FOR WOMAN SUFFRAGE ON ELECTION DAY.

▲ Check out several sources to compare contrasting ideas and get a broader perspective of the subject.

TERTIARY SOURCE

KEY INFORMATION

Democracy is a system of government that believes in the free and equitable right for all citizens to participate in government, either directly or indirectly.

Civil liberties are fundamental rights and freedoms that are granted to everyone in a democracy.

Freedom of the press is the fundamental right for the media, print, electronic, or other forms, to gather and distribute information any way they see fit and without government intervention.

Freedom of expression is the right for a group or individual to express their ideas, thoughts, opinions, and beliefs without fear of censorship or **repercussion**.

> *I always recommend navigating the landscape and understanding where it's coming from, so don't get your media from just one source; get it from a variety of different sources but understand the bias and the source.*
>
> Abby Martin, U.S. journalist and activist

▼ A protest brochure can be a source of information.

To evaluate whether an information source is reliable, you can start with the CRAAP test. CRAAP stands for currency, relevance, authority, accuracy, and purpose, and it's a guide you can use to assess information and build context.

Currency
How current is the information? When was it created, and has it been updated? Are there more recent facts and figures? Is it outdated? Can you still access the links or references provided?

Relevance
Is the information relevant to your needs? Does it help answer your question or tell you what you need to know?

Authority
Who created the information? Does this person or group have any **credentials** or expertise in the subject? Are they closely associated with any businesses or organizations?

Accuracy
Where did the information come from? Can you verify it against other sources? Is it free of errors, such as grammar and spelling mistakes? Does it cite fact-based evidence and provide references?

Purpose
Why was the source created? Was it intended to sway the reader? Does the source have a strong point of view or opinion?

BIAS IN INFORMATION

Bias is when someone has an opinion in favor of or against a person, group, or thing. In most cases, bias is unconscious, and the person is not aware of it. However, it can still be harmful because it affects everything we see and do. Everyone has bias—it's a natural part of being human. As a result, all sources of information—present and past—have bias of some kind. Some try to stay neutral and remove their bias from content they create. Others might purposefully express biased points of view as a way to sway others to their side.

To assess the credibility of information, you need to know how to detect bias. Ask these questions when evaluating information:

- Who is the creator? Are they being paid to express their point of view? Do they have a political connection or an **agenda** to fulfill?
- Does the creator only present one side of a debate or express strong opinions or beliefs?
- Is there evidence to back up any claims the creator makes? Can you find other information sources to support them? Does the creator omit facts or use them selectively?
- What is the tone? Does the creator try to make you feel a certain way? Do they use strong or inappropriate language?

ASK YOUR OWN QUESTIONS

Are you aware of any biases you might have? How do they affect the way you think or feel about an issue? Have you ever come across information that is obviously biased? How can biased information be useful? Should all biases be removed from content? Why?

▲ Bias can lead you to look or trust information that supports what you already believe.

3 WHERE INFORMATION COMES FROM

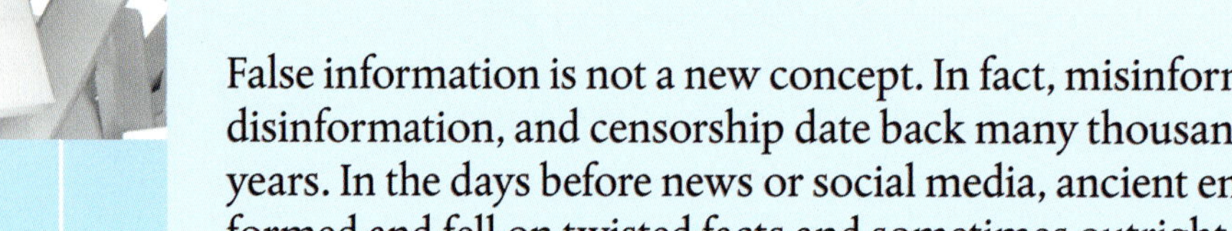

False information is not a new concept. In fact, misinformation, disinformation, and censorship date back many thousands of years. In the days before news or social media, ancient empires formed and fell on twisted facts and sometimes outright lies.

About 2,000 years ago, ancient Rome was in a state of civil war. Roman ruler Octavian was **consolidating** power and set his sights on eliminating onetime ally and co-ruler Mark Antony. Both used ancient forms of misinformation and disinformation to sway the Roman people to their side. In the end, Octavian won both the physical war and the **propaganda** war. He said Mark Antony was not to be trusted because he abandoned Rome to live with his lover, Egyptian Queen Cleopatra. He said Mark Antony was more loyal to her than to the people of Rome. Cleopatra in particular was portrayed as using her beauty to trick Antony. Facts show she was smart, well-educated, and ordinary-looking. Her intelligence and charm won people over.

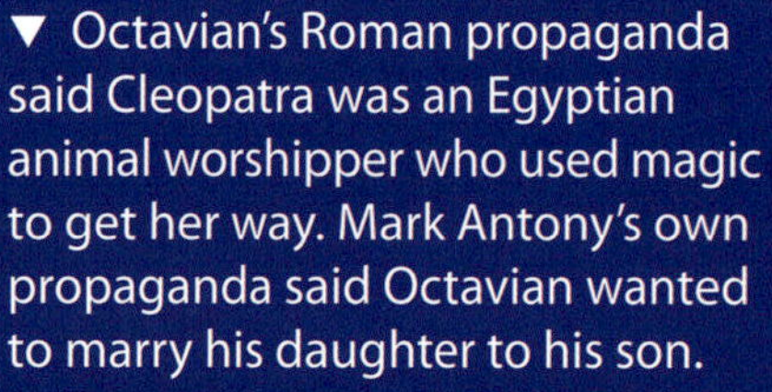

▼ Octavian's Roman propaganda said Cleopatra was an Egyptian animal worshipper who used magic to get her way. Mark Antony's own propaganda said Octavian wanted to marry his daughter to his son.

► Octavian became Augustus, the first Roman emperor, after eliminating all his opponents.

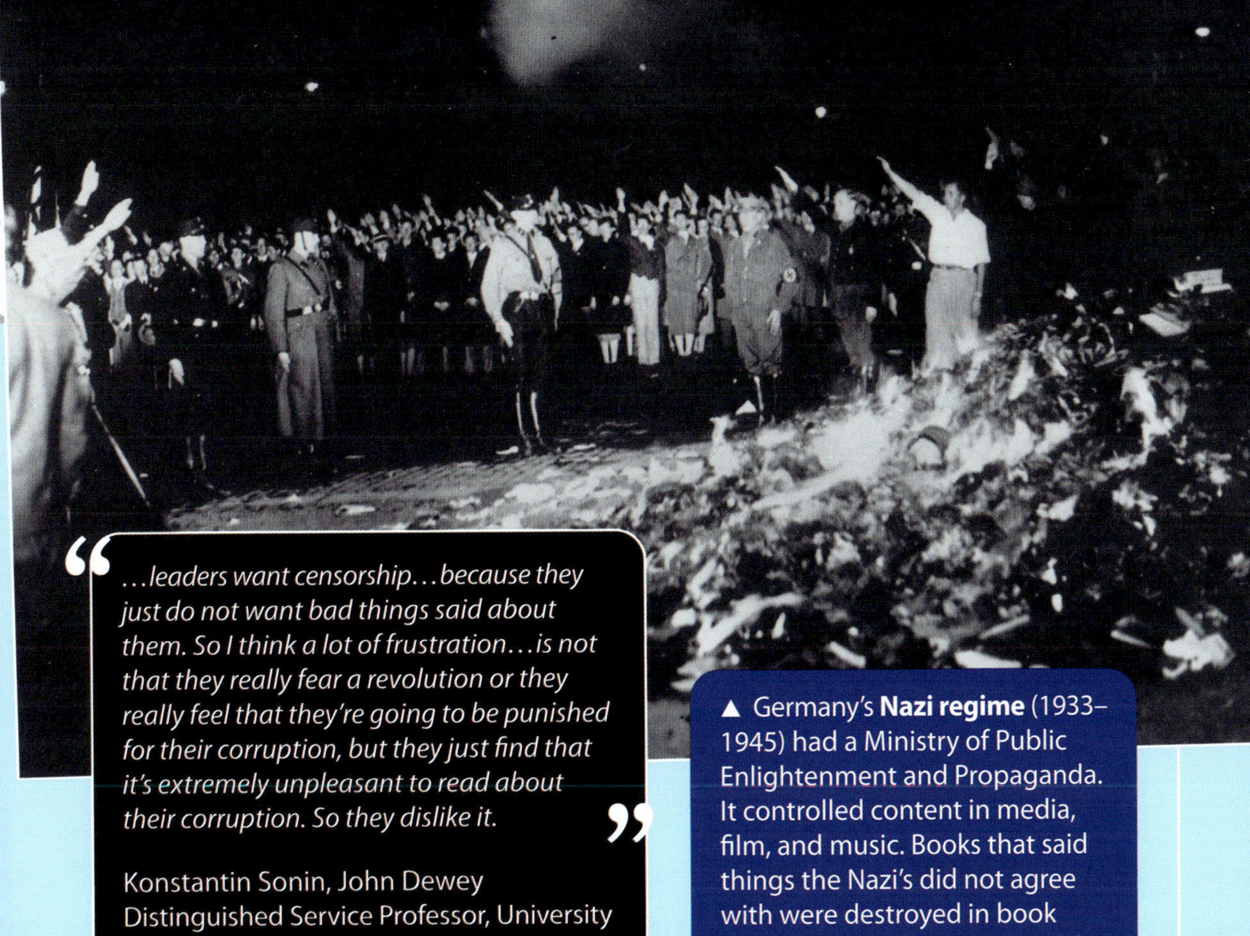

> *...leaders want censorship...because they just do not want bad things said about them. So I think a lot of frustration...is not that they really fear a revolution or they really feel that they're going to be punished for their corruption, but they just find that it's extremely unpleasant to read about their corruption. So they dislike it.*
>
> Konstantin Sonin, John Dewey Distinguished Service Professor, University of Chicago Harris School of Public Policy

▲ Germany's **Nazi regime** (1933–1945) had a Ministry of Public Enlightenment and Propaganda. It controlled content in media, film, and music. Books that said things the Nazi's did not agree with were destroyed in book burnings attended by the public.

During the American Civil War in the 1860s, the federal, or Union, government placed limitations on the freedom of the press and freedom of speech. Reporters were censored from writing negative stories about the draft or discouraging people from **enlisting**, and they could be arrested if they disobeyed.

Throughout the 1930s, the Nazi regime in Germany encouraged students to burn books they felt were not German in spirit, such as those by Jewish **intellectuals** Albert Einstein and Sigmund Freud. German **dictator** Adolf Hitler and the Nazis used propaganda to influence the thoughts and feelings of German people. They fed into common **stereotypes** and used art, music, theater, films, books, radio, educational materials, and the press to spread disinformation and untruths that led to the **genocide** of millions of Jews across Europe.

These are just a few examples of how misinformation, disinformation, and censorship have shaped people's points of view and beliefs throughout history. There are countless other examples of false information in world history.

OTHER INFORMATION SOURCES

If misinformation, disinformation, and censorship have always been around, why is it such an important topic today? Information comes from a wide variety of places. YouTube videos, posters on the walls at school, conversations around the dinner table, and e-mail newsletters from your favorite store are just a few ways you might receive information on a daily basis. Other information sources are more formal, such as newspaper articles or scholarly journals. Understanding the different types of information sources and their advantages or disadvantages can help you recognize misinformation, disinformation, and censorship, and understand how it spreads.

▼ Google Scholar is a website where anyone can search for scholarly articles.

COMPUTER MEDIA

PRINT MEDIA

BROADCAST MEDIA

"Media" is a general term used to describe all channels of mass communication, including broadcasting, publishing, music, art, video games, phones, and the Internet. The word media can be used to refer to both the content and the device that delivers the content. The following are four main types of media with examples of how people use them to communicate:

Print media

Print media is the oldest form of media. It includes publications that are physically printed on paper, such as newspapers, magazines, brochures, books, billboards, advertisements, and more.

Broadcast media

Broadcast media includes radio and television, which are used to broadcast sounds and images in a way that entertains, informs, and educates.

Digital media

Digital media refers to the Internet as well as all the websites, blogs, podcasts, streaming services, and other content found on the Internet. Spotify and Netflix are examples of digital media that compete with traditional broadcast media.

Computer media

Computer media refers to USB drives, memory cards, hard drives, compact discs (CDs), and other types of computer hardware that are used to store information. Computer media is starting to replace print media. People often use eReaders that can store thousands of books on a single device, or look at photos on their phones instead of printing them and putting them into a physical album.

DIGITAL MEDIA

"Social media" refers to applications and websites that allow people to collaborate, connect, and share information in real time. People can post almost anything they want on social media, and their followers will see it. There are certain restrictions. For example, content that includes hate speech or nudity or messages that are considered **harassment** can be reported by users and blocked by the platform.

▲ Some social media apps encourage followers who have similar viewpoints. Others claim to promote free speech.

MISINFORMATION SPREAD

The rise of social media plays a big part in the spread of false information. It spreads faster than it did in the past because so many people all over the world are connected through social media. It's also obvious when information is omitted or censored because people have access to so many different information sources.

Once content is put online in the form of a post, tweet, reel, or story, it can easily be viewed, liked, and shared by people everywhere, not just the people you come into contact with in your daily life. In general, you can expect your followers to see your content, as well as your followers' followers, and people who follow any hashtags you add to your content. This concept is known as "**organic** reach." The more people engage with social media content, the more likely it is to be recommended to other users of the social media platform. In a matter of minutes, the information might be seen by thousands of people all over the world.

ALGORITHMS

Social media platforms use mathematical **equations** called "**algorithms**" to organize content on individual users' feeds. The platform can tailor the accounts and content you see, based on your interactions, such as likes, comments, and shares. The idea is to filter out content you might not like or that you might find irrelevant. However, this can also mean you miss out on seeing content that could give you a more balanced perspective of the world. People with larger followings and more engagement have a farther reach than others. In this way, social media censors what you see by promoting some content and omitting other content on your feed.

▼ Hashtags bring awareness to important social movements. In 2022, a young Iranian woman was killed by police in that country for not wearing hijab in accordance to government standards. Her name became one of the most repeated hashtags of the year #MahsaAmini. It called worldwide attention to the protests against her death.

There are also times when the speed of social media can be damaging. A 2018 study conducted by MIT scholars concluded that fake news travels much faster on social media than factual information. In fact, false stories are 70 percent more likely to be retweeted on Twitter than true stories.

ONCE IT IS OUT THERE...

Once a post goes **viral** on social media, it's hard to take it back because it spreads quickly. For example, in April 2018, 10 people were killed and more than a dozen injured when a man drove his van into a crowd of people in Toronto, Canada. People began to speculate whether the attack might be an act of terrorism.

Journalist Natasha Fatah arrived on the scene and reported eyewitness accounts. Two tweets posted just 30 minutes apart provided different descriptions of the attacker's identity. The first tweet wrongfully identified the attacker as a Middle Eastern man, while the second tweet correctly described the driver of the van as a white man. Immediately, the misinformation received more engagement than the factual tweet. Weeks later, people were still sharing the false information and incorrectly linking the attack to Middle Eastern **extremists**.

◄ A memorial set up for the victims of the attack includes condolences in different languages and scripts, and a "hatred for none" theme to counteract false information.

GOVERNMENT INFO

Governments often create or compile information for public consumption. It might include laws, policies, statistics, research studies, technical papers, financial reports, presidential documents, official statements, and expert testimonials. Government information can be a useful and relevant source for both current and historical content.

Access to government information is a cornerstone of democracy. It allows people to make informed decisions and hold the government accountable for its actions. The government has a responsibility to provide information to the public. In general, government information in democratic countries is considered reliable and credible. Nearly 130 countries have freedom of information laws and about 50 constitutions recognize it as a right. In the United States, the Freedom of Information Act ensures the general public can access government records.

Not all government information is publicly available, though. The government controls access to sensitive information, such as documents that contain details about weapons of mass destruction, **trade secrets**, or military activities. If this kind of information fell into enemy hands, it could become a security threat. Personal information is also often restricted.

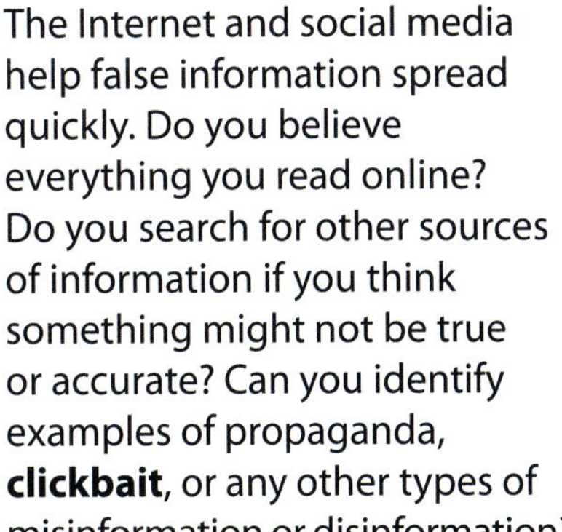

THE CENTRAL ISSUES

The Internet and social media help false information spread quickly. Do you believe everything you read online? Do you search for other sources of information if you think something might not be true or accurate? Can you identify examples of propaganda, **clickbait**, or any other types of misinformation or disinformation? Where were they? How did they make you feel?

▼ The National Archives and Records Administration is an "independent federal agency of the United States government within the executive branch," charged with the preservation and documentation of government and historical records.

Governments regulate information to ensure it is used in ways that will not cause harm to others. In Canada and the United States, there are many privacy laws that govern how businesses use the information they collect from individuals. For instance, banks collect personal information to provide loans, mortgages, and other services, and medical centers store individual health records. All this information is protected and can only be used for the **explicit** purposes for which it was collected.

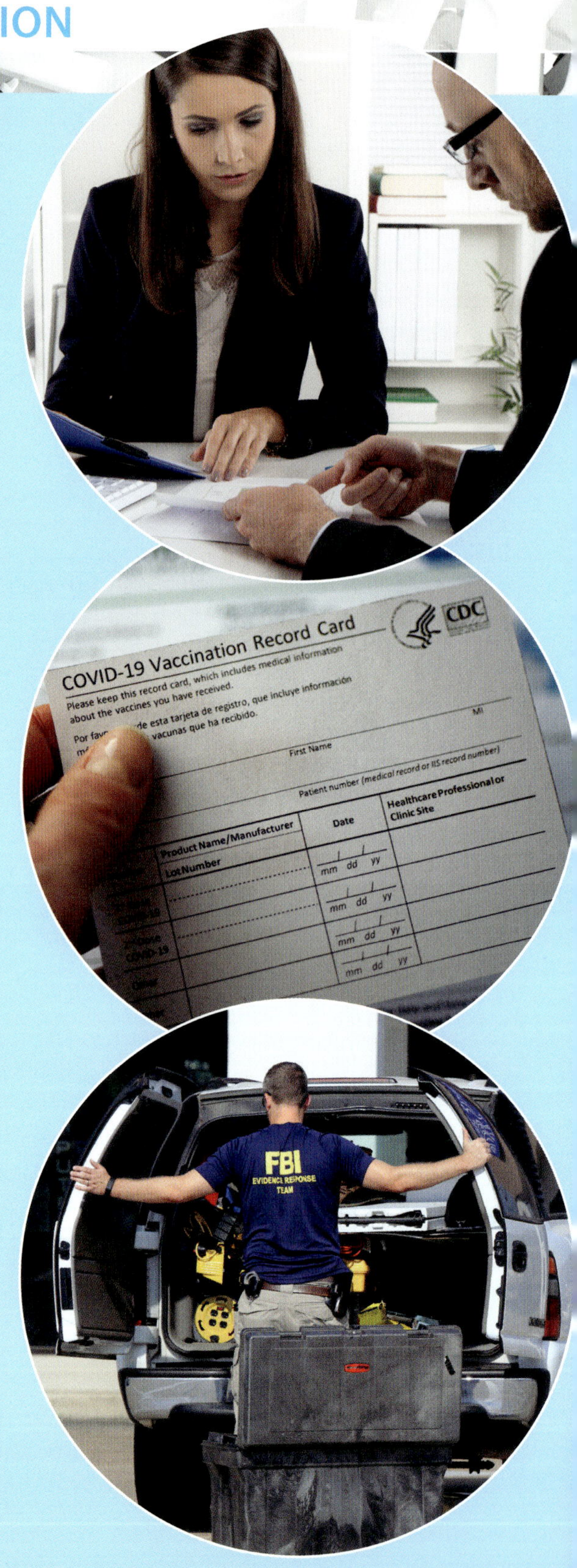

MONITORING INFO

Governments sometimes monitor information to assist with criminal investigations, detect threats such as terror plots, or gain a deeper understanding of breaking events. In the United States, the Department of Homeland Security, the Federal Bureau of Investigation (FBI), the State Department, and other federal agencies might use social media to learn more about people, organizations, and current events. In certain situations, they can monitor real-time chats, direct messages, and other private online communications. There are restrictions on the types of information government agencies can monitor and how they use the information.

▲ Countries such as China and Russia are known to control the media as a way to exert political pressure.

CENSORED INFORMATION

Restricting and regulating information for safety or security reasons is not the same as censorship. While some governments use censorship as a form of control over their people, countries such as the United States and Canada must abide by laws and regulations that govern the types of information they can control. For example, in August 2022, former Pakistan prime minister Imran Khan accused the government of Pakistan of censorship, after media outlets, such as YouTube and TV stations, were blocked from airing his live speeches. Khan had spoken critically of the Pakistan government on several occasions. By censoring his speech, the government hoped to discredit Khan and prevent people from thinking negatively about government agencies.

STATE-SPONSORED INFORMATION

Government control of information is also different from state-sponsored information. When a government has control over the media, either directly or indirectly, it is said to be state sponsored. In some cases, the government might implement laws that restrict the freedom of the press. As a result, the media can only provide coverage the government deems appropriate. In other cases, the government might own the media or provide financial support to media outlets. The media is then **indebted** to the government.

▼ In 2020, Twitter started labeling state-sponsored media accounts that use the platform as a way to advance their political agenda and spread disinformation. In the interest of democracy, Twitter also stopped promoting state-sponsored accounts to its users.

One of the best ways to get credible fact-based information on a topic is by listening to what experts have to say about it. While experts will have biases, they aim to present fair, well-researched opinions, facts, and information. Examples of relevant, reliable sources for expert information include:

- Nongovernmental organizations, such as the World Health Organization, United Nations, and World Bank
- Educational institutions, including Harvard, Cambridge, Johns Hopkins, and Massachusetts Institute of Technology (MIT)
- Nonprofit organizations, such as the Red Cross, Greenpeace, and World Wildlife Fund
- Respected professionals, including scientists, researchers, historians, and others with qualifications, credentials, and expertise in specific topics

"*Don't join the book burners. Don't think you are going to conceal faults by concealing the evidence that they ever existed. Don't be afraid to go into your library and read every book.*"

Former U.S. president Dwight Eisenhower

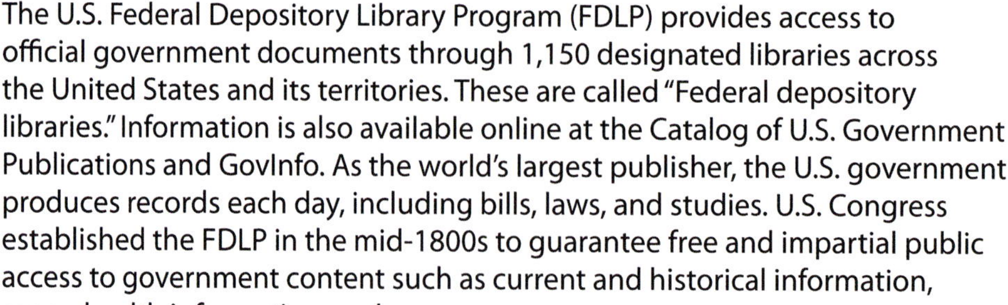

KEY PLAYERS

The U.S. Federal Depository Library Program (FDLP) provides access to official government documents through 1,150 designated libraries across the United States and its territories. These are called "Federal depository libraries." Information is also available online at the Catalog of U.S. Government Publications and GovInfo. As the world's largest publisher, the U.S. government produces records each day, including bills, laws, and studies. U.S. Congress established the FDLP in the mid-1800s to guarantee free and impartial public access to government content such as current and historical information, maps, health information, and more.

PERSONAL OPINIONS

Much of the information you receive comes from friends and family. Their personal experiences and education influence how they interpret events and the way they communicate their thoughts. It is good to hear a variety of opinions and points of view about a topic, especially if they are different from your own. However, unless your friends and family are experts on the topic, they might be spreading misinformation. If they are very passionate about the topic, they might even spread disinformation as a way to sway you to their side. Watch for any bias that might make its way into your conversations, and verify any facts using credible sources.

4 HOW TO ASSESS INFORMATION

We know that misinformation and disinformation can spread through media, social media, and conversations with friends and family. But what does it look like? How can you recognize content that is untrue—intentional or otherwise? How do you know if information is censored? Is it being kept from you entirely, or has there been an intentional omission of certain details?

INFORMATION LITERACY

When information comes at you from all angles all day long, you need to make quick decisions about whether it is accurate, credible, and complete. You need to use your time wisely and effectively. Developing information literacy skills can help you recognize when you need information and how to locate, evaluate, and use the information in a way that gets you what you need quickly and efficiently.

> *"When we hear new information, we often think about what it may mean. If we later hear a correction, it doesn't invalidate our thoughts—and it's our own thoughts that can maintain a bias, even when we accept that the original information was false."*
>
> Norbert Schwarz, PhD, a professor of psychology and marketing at the University of Southern California

There are five key skills involved in information literacy:

1. ***Identify***
   What is it that you need to know? Are you writing an essay about climate change for your social studies class? Do you want to know which dog breed is best for your family? Begin by identifying the topic that you want to know more about.

2. ***Locate***
   What is the fastest, easiest way to find the information you need to answer your questions? Official websites for organizations such as the United Nations Climate Action or the American Kennel Club might be a good place to start.

3. ***Evaluate***
   Are the information sources credible and reliable? Can you verify the facts elsewhere? Do they contain obvious bias? Look to see if the websites have been updated with the most recent information.

4. ***Acknowledge***
   How can you apply the information? Are there images you can download to use in a visual presentation on climate change or dog breeds?

5. ***Apply***
   Were the images you used without **copyright**? Have you been careful not to copy it as if it was your own? What do you need to do to properly credit the sources you used? You might include a bibliography in your essay or give credit to any dog images on your poster.

Misinformation and disinformation campaigns are designed to make people think emotionally instead of critically. For instance, if something makes a person fear they might be in danger, it can appeal to their personal biases and influence their decisions. This explains why, despite scientific evidence, some people deny that climate change is real or that vaccines are effective.

Even long after misinformation has been disproven, doubts can linger. For this reason, it is even more important than ever to evaluate information carefully before making any decisions or forming an opinion.

Evaluating information is not a skill that comes naturally. It requires work to analyze and evaluate information and determine what is relevant. One of the reasons why people doubt science is because science continually reevaluates evidence. What scientists believed before may change based on evidence that can be tested.

▼ Sometimes people don't trust information because the source of the information has misled people before. That's why it's important to check multiple sources using a reliable method.

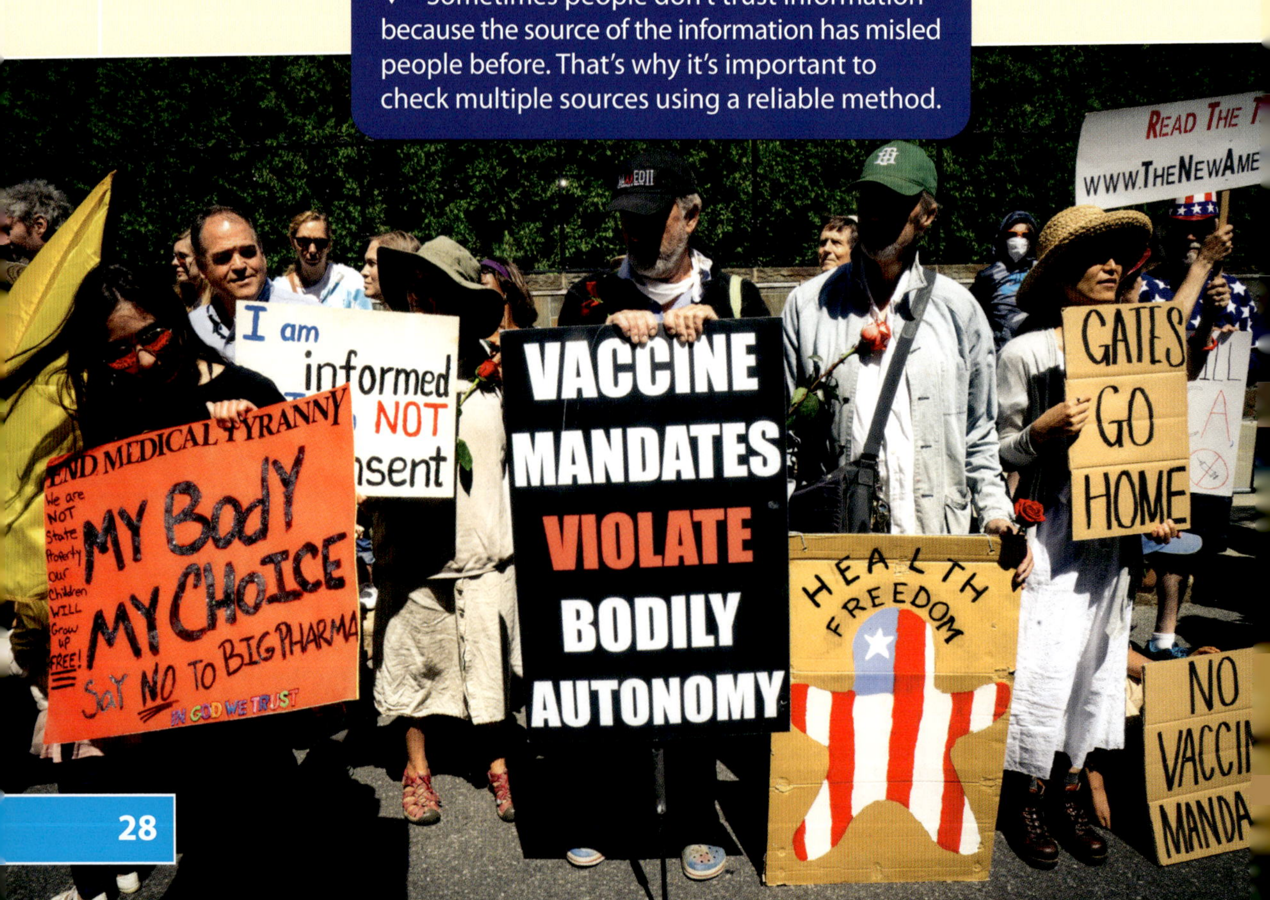

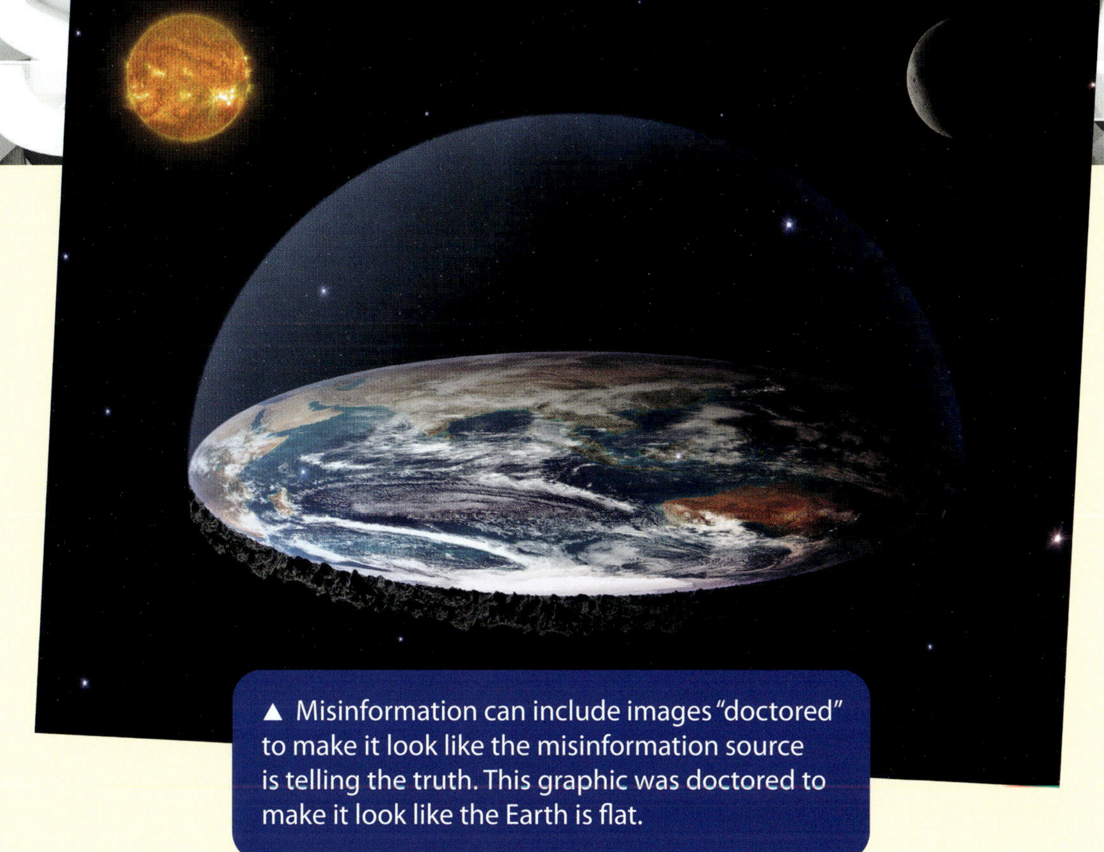

▲ Misinformation can include images "doctored" to make it look like the misinformation source is telling the truth. This graphic was doctored to make it look like the Earth is flat.

THE SIFT METHOD

The SIFT Method is a series of four actions that can be used to help determine if a source of information is reliable:

1. ***Stop***. Before you do anything, stop and ask if you know and trust the website. If not, use the next three steps to decide if you should trust it before you continue.
2. ***Investigate the source***. Decide whether the source is worth your time and effort. Look at who sponsored or created the content. What was their purpose and intent? Does the content make **logical** sense?
3. ***Find a better source***. After performing steps 1 and 2, you might decide the source is not trustworthy or worth your time. It's best to stop investing any more effort into it and find a better source.
4. ***Trace claims, quotes, and media to their origin***. Sometimes, information is taken out of context. Part of a quote is removed or a video is edited to make it seem like something it's not. Check any links or references to ensure the information is accurately represented.

Well-balanced, evidence-based sources of information present a topic from every angle. They highlight the facts fairly and accurately and prevent bias as much as possible. However, some information sources are designed to mislead their audiences. They are intentionally biased and represent a specific point of view. In some cases, it is very clear that the source is promoting a certain concept or idea. In other cases, it's not as obvious. The audience needs to stay focused to recognize it for what it is—false information.

Information literacy skills help assess whether information fits into several types of misinformation or disinformation:

Propaganda

If you have ever seen a poster of Uncle Sam or Rosie the Riveter, you've seen propaganda. These characters were created to recruit men into the army in World War I and women as defense workers in World War II. Propaganda uses select facts and half-truths to manipulate people's beliefs and behaviors. It can include posters, videos, flyers, music, artwork, and more. Propaganda usually promotes a political agenda, and it targets specific groups and individuals.

▲ A World War II German propaganda poster

> *[Propaganda's] task is not to make an objective study of the truth, in so far as it favors the enemy, and then set it before the masses with academic fairness; its task is to serve our own right, always and unflinchingly.*
>
> Adolf Hitler

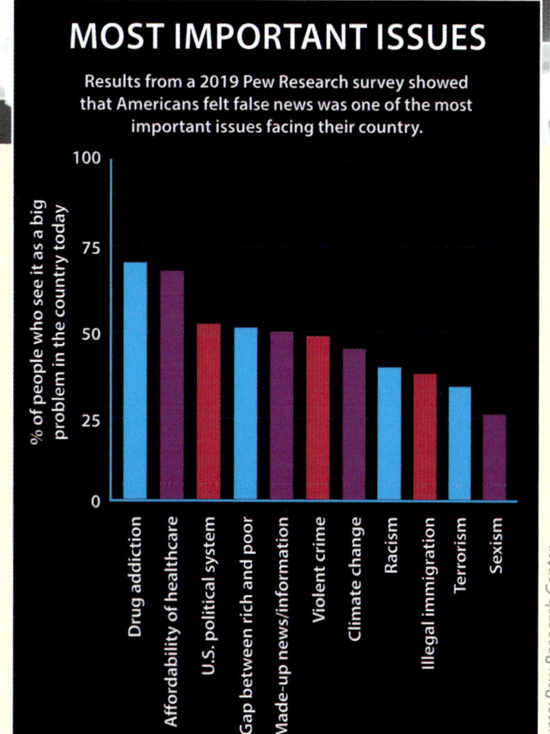

Fake news

Have you ever come across a website that looked very similar to one you know and trust, but something about it didn't seem right? It might have been an **imposter** trying to **dupe** you. Fake news outlets work the same way. They mimic trusted websites and credible content creators by **spoofing** their domain names or impersonating their style. They present false information and, often, the content is entirely fiction. In 2016, fake news quickly spread that Democratic presidential candidate Hillary Clinton was at the helm of a child trafficking ring operating at a pizza place in Washington, DC. The fake news story, known as Pizzagate, was fabricated to deter voters from electing Clinton as president.

Conspiracy theories

When someone suggests that a major event is the secret plot of a powerful person or group that has **nefarious** intentions, they are likely sharing a conspiracy theory. Most conspiracy theories are based on opinions and ideas instead of facts. Two common conspiracy theories are that the British royal family had Princess Diana run off the road and killed, and that the CIA assassinated former U.S. president John F. Kennedy, not Lee Harvey Oswald.

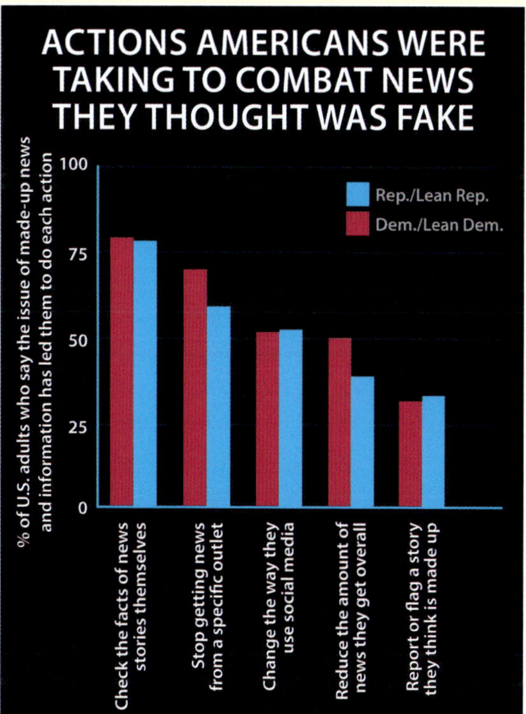

Deepfakes

Have you ever seen a video of a celebrity or politician doing something completely out of character? Deepfake technology uses deep learning artificial intelligence to swap a person's face with someone else's face. In 2019, a video was released that showed Facebook CEO Mark Zuckerburg bragging about how he could control people's lives through their stolen data. This is just one example of a deepfake. Zuckerberg never said those words.

Clickbait

If you have ever read a headline that was so compelling you had to read the rest of the story, it might have been clickbait. **Sensational** headlines are one of the tactics marketers use to tempt people into clicking a link and consuming their content. The goal is to grab attention and appeal to a person's natural curiosity. Clickbait often uses phrases like "You'll Never Believe…" or "X Things You Need to Know About…" Getting people to click is the most important thing. Clickbait is often associated with fake news or poor-quality products that do not deliver on their promises.

SOCIAL BOTS

Automated programs called "social bots" are designed to mimic human behavior on social media. They are used by marketers and political groups to quickly spread information. They can take part in discussions, create content, and like or share posts without any human involvement. Trolls are humans who intentionally **provoke** online conflicts by posting nasty comments and messages. They often twist people's words to make them upset. They might even bully or harass others.

▼ Clickbait is designed to make people "click."

DESIGNED FOR ANGER

False information creates an emotional response in people by appealing to them in some way. It might make a person so angry that they can't hold back their thoughts. It might also make them sad and want to show their sympathy by spreading the word. Most people share misinformation by accident. As they scroll through their social media, they make quick decisions about the information, then repost it without much thought. They don't realize the information is false because they aren't paying close attention to it, not because they can't tell the difference between what is real and what is fake.

Only a small percentage of people spread disinformation, and they typically do it for the purpose of causing harm. They target specific individuals with their campaigns and try to manipulate their thoughts. Content is designed to play into the biases of people or groups who share beliefs or values. In many cases, disinformation includes **slanderous** or hate speech that is not considered legal or fair. It is often used to drive extreme viewpoints, divide people, and push them away from each other instead of promoting healthy debate.

LOW RISK — HIGH RISK

WHAT'S AT STAKE?

Misinformation, disinformation, and censorship can cause people to make poor choices. Which one do you think is more damaging? Why? Do you think people need to watch for false or omitted information in everything they do or only at certain times?

▲ In 2020, bushfires ripped through parts of Australia that were largely the result of climate change. People who wanted to deflect attention from the climate crisis falsely claimed the fires were the result of arson. Disinformation and misinformation about the root cause of the disaster quickly grew out of control.

5 STAYING INFORMED

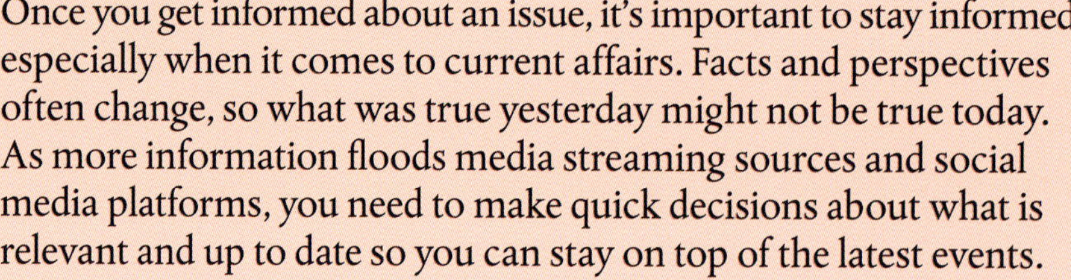

Once you get informed about an issue, it's important to stay informed, especially when it comes to current affairs. Facts and perspectives often change, so what was true yesterday might not be true today. As more information floods media streaming sources and social media platforms, you need to make quick decisions about what is relevant and up to date so you can stay on top of the latest events.

DISINFORMATION FOR HIRE

People with dishonest intent often find new ways to spread disinformation. Some hire social media influencers and public relations firms to help promote their cause. In May 2021, several French and German influencers received an offer from a London-based public relations agency called Fazze. It promised to pay them a large fee in exchange for posting unsupported claims about the number of deaths linked to the BioNTech-Pfizer COVID-19 vaccine. The influencers could not say they were being paid for the post and had to pretend it was their personal opinion. Many questioned the **ethics** of the offer and declined. It was later discovered that Fazze was not a real agency. The offer came from sources aiming to discredit European- and American-produced vaccines as a way to increase the popularity of the Russian Sputnik V vaccine.

> *People are often capable of distinguishing between true and false news content, but fail to even consider whether content is accurate before they share it on social media.*
>
> Gordon Pennycook, assistant professor of behavioral science at the University of Regina

◄ YouTube creators earn money if they have at least 1,000 subscribers and 4,000 watch hours in a year. This is an incentive to create content that gets a lot of clicks.

▲ Free media, or a free press, means people and the press can express ideas that not everyone agrees with. But that doesn't mean people are free to spread misinformation and disinformation without **checks and balances**.

IMPORTANCE OF FREE PRESS

Article 19 of the Universal Declaration of Human Rights states that "Everyone has the right to freedom of opinion and expression." This right includes the freedom to hold opinions without interference, and to look for and read information through any media. The idea behind a free press is that everyone can express their opinions and ideas—even if they go against the government—without the fear of **punishment**.

Most democratic countries include freedom of the press and freedom of expression in their constitutional rights. They are included in the First Amendment of the United States and the Charter of Rights and Freedoms in Canada. Freedom of the press and freedom of expression serve as checks and balances. When people have the right to speak openly about issues, including criticizing the government and large businesses or organizations, they can help prevent any one group from exerting too much power.

With a free press, people can access more and different sources of information, including independent media outlets that report on the actions of governments and elected representatives as a way to hold them accountable. This helps people to be informed about important issues and events that might affect their lives, such as criminal activities or threats to the environment.

PRESS LIMITATIONS

Some countries have limited free press or no free press at all. For example, the North Korean constitution includes the rights to free press and freedom of expression, but there are tight government controls on the distribution of information and independent journalism is prohibited. In Hungary, the media is largely state owned, and independent media outlets must comply with government regulations about what they can report.

▲ North Korea is a **totalitarian dictatorship** ruled by one family that also controls the one political party. All media, including the main television channel, Korean Central Television, is controlled by that one party.

WITHOUT FREE PRESS

When there is no free press, people do not get a clear picture of events. Some facts might be manipulated or censored to paint the group or person that owns the media outlet in a more favorable light. Other times, news reports might contain false or misleading information that tries to make readers and viewers feel a certain way about the owner of the media outlet or to discredit its competitors.

Social media has made it hard for small, independent news outlets to remain in business. The number of readers and viewers is declining because people consume a large amount of information online instead. Most social media shares information at no cost to the user.

▲ While private media operates fairly freely in Poland, a state-owned company owns and controls many regional newspapers. The largest private media group is faced with special legislation and regulations that limit its reach.

FURTHER RESEARCH

Since freedom of the press and freedom of expression are not always guaranteed, it is critical to look at social and political issues from different angles. One way to do this is through triangulation, or the use of multiple sources to verify or cross-check information. Triangulation helps reduce bias and ensure information is correct so people can form a comprehensive understanding of an issue.

Data triangulation
The comparison of various data sources to validate findings and reduce false information.

Methods triangulation
The use of different methods to perform a study, which helps minimize biases and **deficiencies** that might happen in any of the individual studies.

Investigator triangulation
The involvement of more than one investigator, which might be a researcher, interviewer, or other specialization, to add credibility and decrease bias.

Theory triangulation
The use of different theories to analyze the situation, which might include asking different types of questions or looking at the situation from different points of view.

> *"There has been more new error propagated by the press in the last ten years than in an hundred years before 1798."*
>
> Former U.S. president John Adams

Non-partisan groups and organizations have no political affiliations. They operate independently and objectively to do research studies, analyze content, and conduct surveys and public opinion polls. Their goal is to offer an impartial view of key issues, attitudes, and trends that shape society as a whole. This allows the public to make informed decisions.

THE CENTRAL ISSUES

Most media outlets in the United States and Canada operate without any political pressure. They are free to report the truth, even if it portrays the government and political figures negatively. Why is this important in a democracy? On the other hand, in communist China, there is no free press, content is heavily censored, and journalists are often harassed and detained. How might the lack of access to independent information sources affect the way people make decisions in China or how they feel about certain issues?

▼ Public Agenda and Pew Research are examples of non-partisan research groups.

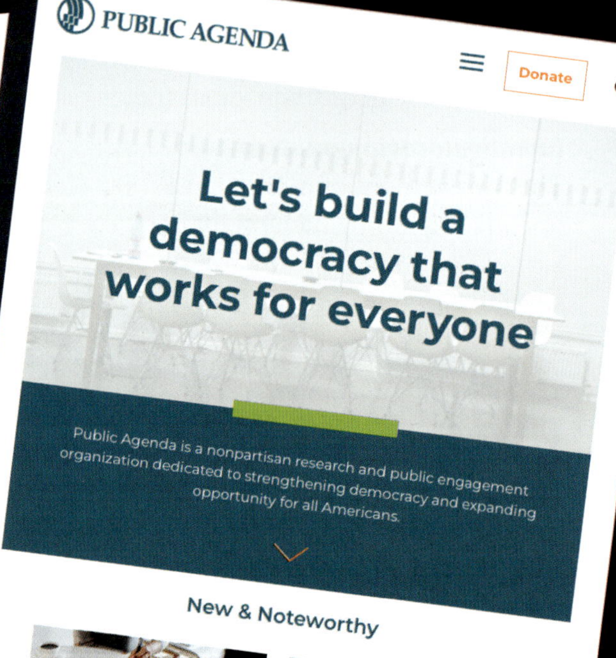

KEY PLAYERS

The U.S. Agency for Global Media (USAGM) connects and informs people who support liberal democracy and freedom of information, especially those living in places that lack free press. Formerly known as the Broadcasting Board of Governors, the USAGM is an independent agency of the U.S. government that oversees all U.S. and international media. It provides funding to media outlets that provide information, such as Voice of America, Radio Free Europe/Radio Liberty, Radio Free Asia, the Office of Cuba Broadcasting, and the Middle East Broadcasting Networks. Each week, the USAGM spans more than 100 countries, reaching about 394 million people in more than 60 languages.

▼ In March 2020, Indian actor Amitabh Bachchan tweeted false information that claimed houseflies spread COVID-19. This graph shows how Google searches for the word "housefly" in English and Hindi spiked following Bachchan's tweet.

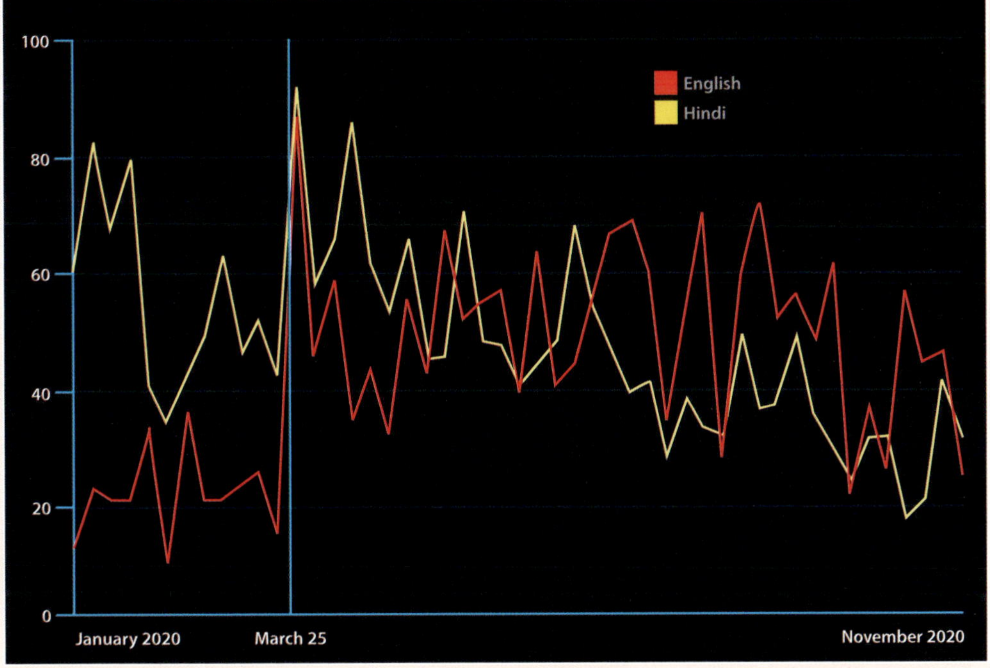

100
80
60
40
20
0
English
Hindi
January 2020
March 25
November 2020

Source: Google Trends data

6 PLAN OF ACTION

Misinformation, disinformation, and censorship can cause people to lose faith in all sources of information, even those that are legitimate and reliable. It is important to know how to recognize when information is questionable. People who are less digitally literate are more likely to spread misinformation and disinformation because they are less likely to know the signs.

> *Diverse books create a better lens through which all children can see themselves in library collections. And yet these very titles—the ones addressing cultural invisibility and cultivating understanding—are the ones that are most frequently challenged.*
>
> ALA President Patricia "Patty" Wong

▲ Public trust in advertising media is often low. Advertising standards organizations help by setting codes for advertisers, and ways for people to complain when ads are misleading.

MEDIA LITERACY

Unlike TV or radio programs that you must tune in to at a particular time, the Internet provides a constant influx of information from across the globe. Media literacy is an essential skill that empowers you to make good choices about the messages you hear or read in the media. It involves using your critical thinking skills to decode media messages and analyze how they want you to feel. Ask the following questions:

- Who created the message? Was it a company, an organization, or an individual? *For example, it might be a beauty company that makes smooth skin face cream.*
- What is the key point of the message? Why did they create it and what do they hope to achieve? Do they want to make you feel a certain way about an issue? *The beauty company might make an ad that entices young women who want smooth skin to buy their product.*
- What does the creator want you to feel? Would someone else feel differently than you? *The beauty company might want women to feel bad if they have blemishes or that their lives won't be as fulfilled.*
- Does the creator use any special techniques to grab your attention? Are there expert testimonials or evidence-based statistics? How do the words and images affect your understanding of the message or how you feel about it? *The beauty company might show pictures of women who don't use their cream looking sad and women using their cream who are happy.*
- Does the creator include certain facts or points of view and omit others? Do you need more information to make a good decision? *The beauty company might present findings from studies that show impressive results after using their product, but might leave out less attractive details about the scent of the cream.*

It is important to understand how the media crafts messages in a way that can influence behaviors and beliefs. Make sure you thoroughly understand an issue before drawing conclusions about it.

Just like the foods you eat need to contain a healthy balance of vegetables, carbohydrates, and proteins, the news you consume needs to be well balanced to make sure you have a healthy view of the world. Follow these steps to create a thoughtful news diet:

1. Start by performing a news **audit**. List all the places you get information over a 24-hour period and how reliable those sources are. Your list might include radio programs, TV shows, newspapers, podcasts, and social media, for example.
2. Next, think about how well each source meets your needs and if you have a solid mix of resources. Is there anything you need to add to your list or remove from it to make it more balanced? Are there too many personal blogs and not enough public newspapers, for example? Do they contain political bias? Is there more entertainment than news you can use?
3. After a week, look back on the changes you made. Does your new news diet meet your needs? Are you consuming too much news or not enough? Are there any other changes you need to make?

SEARCH TIPS

In search windows on the Internet:

- Use quotation marks around a phrase to find that exact combination of words (for example, "nonviolent protests").
- Use the minus sign to eliminate certain words from your search (for example, protests -violence).
- Use a colon and an extension to search a specific site (for example, protests:.gov for all government website mentions of the topic).
- Use the word "define" and a colon to search for word definitions (for example, Define: social movement).

When looking at websites, address extensions can help identify the sources of the information:
.gov (government)—official government organizations or departments. You may not be able to access all areas of these websites.
.org (organization)—usually nonprofit organizations and charities. You may have to register to use these.
.com (commercial)—mostly businesses. It is the most widely used web address extension.
Country extensions:
.ca Canada
.us United States
.au Australia
.uk United Kingdom
.ru Russia
.de Germany

▼ In 2021, the American Library Association received a record-breaking 729 challenges to ban university, school, and library books, which is a form of censorship. Most of the books challenged were about Black or LGBTQI+ people.

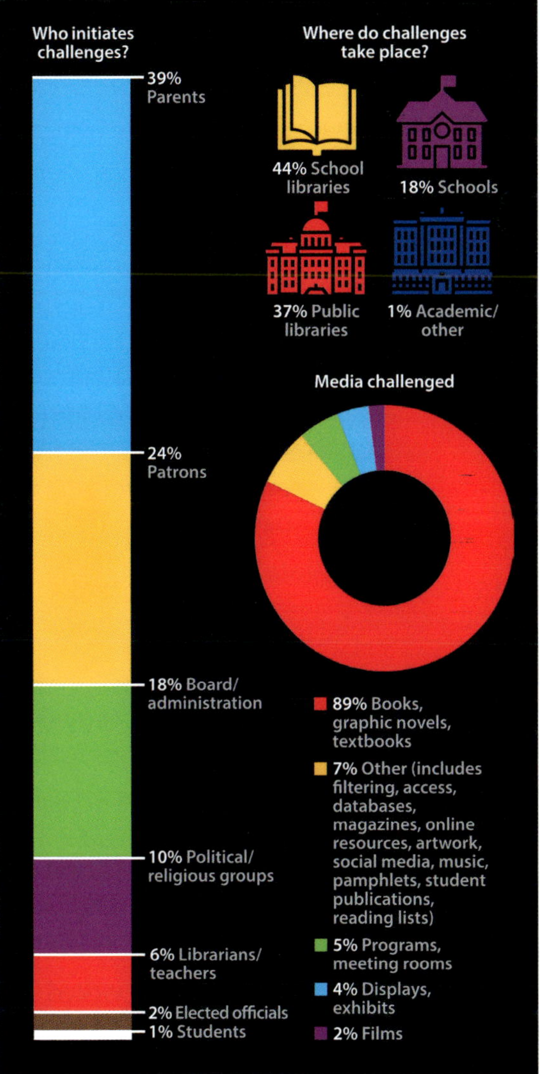

Source: Office for Intellectual Freedom, American Library Association

KEY INFORMATION

The following organizations are working to counter misinformation, disinformation, and censorship:

- Google News Initiative
- Poynter's MediaWise Teen Fact-Checking Network
- TELUS Wise
- FactCheck.org
- Snopes
- TheTrustProject.org
- PolitiFact

If you are ever unsure about whether facts are missing from a news story or a post you read on social media contains false information, you can visit these sites to confirm if the information is true or false.

GOING FORWARD

Getting informed and staying informed can help prevent the spread of misinformation and disinformation and open your eyes to censorship. Using a variety of sources to evaluate an issue, and listening to multiple perspectives, can help you identify false information or the omission of details or facts.

GLOSSARY

abolition The act of stopping something, such as enslavement

agenda Plans or goals that are kept secret

algorithms Instructions or rules used to solve mathematical problems

audit A formal inspection or examination

checks and balances Measures ensuring that no one person, business, or political party gains too much power

civil liberties Fundamental rights and freedoms that all citizens are guaranteed by law or constitution

clickbait A sensational headline that tempts people to click on it and often leads to misleading or false information

consolidating To make something strong by bringing it together as one

copyright The right of a creator to exclusive control over their works

credentials Qualifications, experience, or abilities in a particular field

credible Trustworthy and reliable

deficiencies Insufficient or missing information

dictator A political leader with unlimited governmental power who rules in an oppressive way

dupe To deceive or fool

enlisting Enrolling in the armed forces

equations Mathematical statements of equality or equivalence

explicit Extremely clear and precise

extremists People who hold extreme views or take extreme actions

fraud Any activity based on lies and deceit

genocide Intentional killing of large numbers of people who belong to a certain race, culture, nationality, or religion

harassment The creation of a hostile or unpleasant situation through uninvited or unwelcome verbal or physical conduct

imposter A person who pretends to be someone else

indebted Obligated to provide a service or pay a favor

intellectuals People with a very high intellect

logical Using sound reason and judgment

Nazi regime The far-right National Socialist German Workers' Party that controlled Germany from 1933–1945

nefarious Evil, wicked, or criminal

objectionable Unpleasant or offensive

open source Publicly available and able to be modified

organic Happens naturally and gradually

perspectives Different views on an issue

persuade Make someone do something or feel a certain way by convincing them it's good

prohibition The act of forbidding something, such as alcohol

propaganda Information that is misleading or biased and used to promote a particular political cause or viewpoint

provoke Stir up or cause anger

punishment A penalty given for something said or done

repercussion A negative result or effect produced by an action

sensational Causing, or intending to cause, quick, intense interest, curiosity, or emotional reaction

slanderous Harmful, malicious, and often untrue

spoofing Pretending to be something it's not

stereotypes Unfair or untrue ideas and beliefs about a particular group of people

suffrage The right to vote

suppressing Stopping something from happening

totalitarian dictatorship A political regime in which one leader has total and strict control over everything in citizen's lives

trade secrets Valuable information, practices, or processes

unprecedented Never happened before

vetted Critically reviewed or evaluated for official approval or acceptance

viral Quickly and widely spread

SOURCE NOTES

QUOTATIONS

Page 5: https://tinyurl.com/2uhrdnxy
Page 7: https://tinyurl.com/33cpjfzv
Page 12: https://tinyurl.com/4vf4x9pm
Page 15: https://tinyurl.com/ycxcj2ws
Page 24: https://bit.ly/2OoVfS4
Page 26: https://tinyurl.com/2twj9vh3
Page 30: https://bit.ly/3YFGfzA
Page 34: https://tinyurl.com/7h9j8ys2
Page 37: https://bit.ly/2AWRgoe
Page 40: https://tinyurl.com/2busczjc

REFERENCES USED FOR THIS BOOK

Chapter 1: Well Informed or Misinformed? pages 4–7
https://tinyurl.com/5f9rapmp
https://tinyurl.com/4pfebm7z
https://tinyurl.com/2v2m86hx
https://tinyurl.com/4ppay77c

Chapter 2: How to Get Informed, pages 8–13
https://tinyurl.com/ydwejesw
https://tinyurl.com/33cpjfzv
https://tinyurl.com/5mzv8rwa
https://tinyurl.com/yckn8524
https://tinyurl.com/2khncyb8
https://tinyurl.com/mry642d4

Chapter 3: Where Information Comes From, pages 14–25
https://tinyurl.com/25t9mvpd
https://tinyurl.com/5n86vkjj
https://tinyurl.com/4ud3yu2k
https://tinyurl.com/2twj9vh3
https://tinyurl.com/ywcukct5
https://tinyurl.com/yre6m6jf
https://tinyurl.com/4666n8jf
https://tinyurl.com/4622xkpd
https://tinyurl.com/bdeb78h9
https://tinyurl.com/yc7jjn5k
https://tinyurl.com/5ykrh2wd
https://tinyurl.com/n4b5t48m
https://tinyurl.com/yr53r9tp
https://tinyurl.com/yf4zksy9
https://tinyurl.com/3y9tjwue
https://tinyurl.com/yckbmbm6
https://tinyurl.com/59brnrz5
https://tinyurl.com/n4b5t48m

Chapter 4: How to Assess Information, pages 26–33
https://tinyurl.com/ye24wdus
https://tinyurl.com/rtwttf4j
https://tinyurl.com/28jnvdzp
https://tinyurl.com/46n4zjvv
https://tinyurl.com/2p922fmz
https://tinyurl.com/5fubwbep
https://tinyurl.com/ypjnm9zm
https://tinyurl.com/khkuhd7j
https://tinyurl.com/muauntk9
https://tinyurl.com/ymb6fkj9
https://tinyurl.com/mpsmdhe7

Chapter 5: Staying Informed, pages 34–39
https://tinyurl.com/2twj9vh3
https://tinyurl.com/2p8jyx89
https://tinyurl.com/4dpbh99r
https://tinyurl.com/475shz5c
https://tinyurl.com/2jk4khtz
https://tinyurl.com/ys492yne

Chapter 6: Plan of Action, pages 40–43
https://tinyurl.com/28t3t24e
https://tinyurl.com/y7jmhdz2
https://tinyurl.com/2z73jbju
https://tinyurl.com/4jw3d234
https://tinyurl.com/y8vvyp9c

ABOUT THE AUTHOR

Heather C. Hudak has written hundreds of children's books on all types of topics. She tries to remain unbiased in her work and present accurate, well-rounded information. When she is not writing, Heather enjoys traveling the world and spending time with her husband and pets at her cabin in the woods.

FIND OUT MORE

Finding good source material on the Internet can sometimes be a challenge. When analyzing how reliable the information is, consider these points:

- Who is the author of the page? Is it an expert in the field or a person who experienced the event?
- Is the site well known and up to date? A page that has not been updated for several years probably has out-of-date information.
- Can you verify the facts with another site? Always double-check information.
- Have you checked all possible sites? Don't just look on the first page a search engine provides.
- Remember to try government sites and research papers.
- Have you recorded website addresses and names? Keep this data so you can backtrack later and verify the information you want to use.

WEBSITES

Stay informed about the state of free press in countries all over the world: **https://rsf.org/en**

Learn more about the U.S. Agency for Global Media (USAGM): **www.usagm.gov**

Get non-partisan facts and research on various current events and issues: **www.pewresearch.org**

Find out all about the Federal Depository Library Program (FDLP): **https://bit.ly/3uJrIG1**

Use these tips from the World Health Organization (WHO) to assess information: **www.who.int/news-room/spotlight/let-s-flatten-the-infodemic-curve**

View examples of propaganda: **www.archives.gov/exhibits/powers-of-persuasion**

BOOKS

Dakers, Diane. *Information Literacy and Fake News*. Crabtree Publishing, 2018.

Jackson, Tom. *Fake News*. QEB Publishing, 2020.

Marcus, Leonard S. *You Can't Say That!: Writers for Young People Talk About Censorship, Free Expression, and the Stories They Have to Tell*. Candlewick Press, 2021.

Ogden, Charlie. *Censorship & Privacy*. Crabtree Publishing, 2018.

Osborne, Linda Barrett. *Guardians of Liberty: Freedom of the Press and the Nature of News*. Abrams Books, 2020.

Yasmin, Dr. Seema. *What the Fact? Finding the Truth in All the Noise*. Simon & Schuster Books for Young Readers, 2022.

INDEX